DARE TO LIVE NOW!

Bruce Larson's DARE TO LIVE NOW!
effectively mirrors the author's fresh approach to Christianity and his extraordinary ability to draw out lay leadership. DARE TO LIVE NOW! is honest and provocative. It should prove a helpful guideline for individuals and small groups.

CATHERINE MARSHALL

DARE TO LIVE NOW!

by

BRUCE LARSON

ZONDERVAN PUBLISHING HOUSE

GRAND RAPIDS, MICHIGAN

INTRODUCTION

Jesus spoke a great deal about this present life and relatively little about our future life. His recurring message was, *"Now is the acceptable hour!"* and *"The Kingdom of God is at hand!"* This book is written in the belief that Jesus Christ can change life here and now for any individual, family, church, or group who will discover how to appropriate the power and love which are His.

The chapters in this book have been written over the past dozen years. Many have already appeared in print as articles, initially in *Faith at Work* Magazine. Each chapter deals with situations or circumstances in life that will be fairly common to most readers. It should also be said that the author does not see himself so much as a writer as he does a clinical observer and reporter of man's needs and God's intervention.

The reader will quickly discover that all of these chapters have a single purpose. That purpose is to be as concretely helpful as possible in presenting the *how* of faith in some of life's most basic situations. While it is true that there is an initial turning point in the life of every Christian, it is also true that there are daily turning points. It is in handling these that a Christian is effective or ineffective, victorious or defeated. The purpose of this book is to make clear at each turning point how a person can lay hold of God's willingness to help and to heal and to guide.

Each chapter of this book is highly personal and reveals much of the author's own search for wholeness, maturity, and integrity. I am grateful to the friends, parishioners, colleagues, and most especially family members who have patiently and lovingly and incisively been used of God in the turning points of my own life to date. Next to the gift of Christ's own friendship and presence, I thank Him most of all for the companions of the way whom He has sent.

BRUCE LARSON

New York City
December, 1965

Contents

DARE TO LIVE NOW!

1. DARE TO LIVE NOW!

Man's Predicament and God's Challenge

LIFE IS MEANT to be an adventure. Thomas Carlyle said about someone, "He was born a man and died a grocer." Sin is not just breaking the law but failing to discover the adventure at the very heart of living.

I know a middle-aged man in Canada who for years carried a little black book in his pocket where he recorded all of the unloving and insensitive things that his wife had done to him over the years.

A tanned New York executive in the advertising field told me that he was retiring prematurely and wanted to spend the rest of his life in a lighthouse. He said, "For thirty years I have been coping with people and I have run out of cope."

A young woman who was devoted to God and who spent much of her time and service in the church and in serving others contracted an illness that kept her in bed for years. She described her condition as, "I couldn't die and I couldn't get well."

A gifted clergyman confided to me one day, "The other

night I woke up and saw my wife sleeping beside me and I realized that there was no way out of our hopeless relationship. Divorce is unthinkable and I don't see how either of us can change. I love her, but I don't know how to live with her."

At a funeral the widow told me that for years her husband slept with the lights on and a radio playing afraid to go to sleep lest he die. His doctor told this man, who weighed three hundred pounds, that unless he dieted his life was in danger. The more he feared death, the more he ate. He died at fifty-five.

A young man from Philadelphia, getting a divorce after three years of marriage, told me, "We thought we were meant for each other. Before we were married she'd go sailing with me and love it, and I used to enjoy going to hear her play in a string quartet. But now I get a headache whenever I hear chamber music and she gets seasick every time we go sailing."

A young suburban mother near Boston confided to a small group that in spite of having five children, "I am not a good mother. I find that I don't enjoy children, not even my own."

A six-foot teen-ager in a Canadian college told several of his roommates and friends, "It comes to me that I love my parents very much and appreciate greatly all they have done for me, but I've never told them so. And I know they love me, but they have never said so."

A New Jersey man in his thirties said, "I am so ashamed of the way I treat my family. Why can't I be the man at home that I want to be?"

An executive returned from a conference on creative relationships sponsored by his company and run by a team of social scientists. "The first question they asked us," he said, "was, 'Tell who you are, apart from your job or title.' I found that I was unable to answer and it scared me."

Who am I? Why do I do the things that I do? Why do

other people do what they do? Is God concerned about me and the trap I am in? If He is, what can He do to help me? These are the most basic questions of life.

In the fifth chapter of the book of John, we find a man trapped by life's circumstances. He had been ill for thirty-eight years and was looking for a cure. He spent his days beside a pool where the sick came from far and near. It was an authentic center of healing like Lourdes today or Ste. Anne de Beaupre or possibly was even the counterpart of one of our large medical clinics.

Jesus saw this place filled with human need. He walked among the patients and stopped beside this man who had been there for the greater part of his life and who had obviously been failed by the best medical and religious knowledge of his time. Jesus asks him an amazing question, "Do you *want* to be healed?" On the surface the question seems irrelevant and unfair. Of course this man wanted to be healed. He had spent most of his life in this place where healings occurred from time to time through the curative waters.

However, instead of a simple yes or no, he says, in essence, "Sir, I perceive by your question that you have entirely missed the point. My problem is that the people I have been counting on to put me into the pool at the right time never seem to show up. They are always late." How much this man sounds like a great many of us when asked about our condition. We say, "You see, it's not my fault. My mother was a neurotic. My father was seldom home. My employers have never appreciated me. My friends have let me down, and my wife doesn't understand me." There is something comfortable about the theory of "environmental conditioning" and even depth psychology that lets us off the hook. By blaming others for our present dilemmas we miss the very key to escape.

The issue as God encounters us in the midst of life's pressing situations is not man's goodness or worthiness, for who is worthy before God and who is good enough?

As Jesus intrudes on this man's life the real question is, does he want to pay the price of being well? Though illness may be a great inconvenience, it has many fringe benefits. Illness can be a way to escape the drudgery of work and the burden of responsibility. Each day this man would watch his friends and contemporaries going off to work in hot fields or stifling shops, while he could lie in the cool of the porch beside the pool and discuss the news of the day with his friends or passers-by.

When he was brought home each night, I'm sure this man got preferential treatment from his family. We all know families in which Father whispers to the children, "Let's not upset Mother; she has one of her migraines." By being ill we can often get our way with people who would resist us if we competed on an equal basis.

Self-indulgence can be another fringe benefit. Things that we would not condone in others, we can excuse in ourselves if we are ill, in pain, or incapacitated. Illness is also a way of getting attention, sympathy, or praise.

These suggest some of the things that may be involved in any illness. We can never assume that someone who is ill has an undivided desire to recover. Jesus simply asks this man if he dares to receive the gift of wholeness and begin to live and compete in the world on an equal basis. At some point in this dialogue (which is certainly not recorded in its entirety), the man by the pool must have answered "yes." He is healed, picks up his bedroll, and walks into a new way of life. How different his experience was from that of the woman hypochondriac who, when she died, had carved on her tombstone, "Now will you believe I was sick?"

In trying to understand the human predicament, we see, first, that all of us are being trapped by life in some hopeless situation that can stifle all joy and adventure and fulfillment. No one is immune. On the other hand, we believe in God's love for us, which is not conditioned by our goodness, and His power to release us and transform us. The basic question is, what are the things in us that prevent or block this healing and release?

An experience of mine during World War II has given me some helpful insights into our common predicament. I was a new infantry recruit at Fort Benning, Georgia. When I sat down to my first breakfast in the mess hall, with ten other men at a family style table, I saw something in a large bowl that looked like cream of wheat. I scooped up a large amount in a bowl and poured on milk and sugar. A tall mountain boy sitting across from me was bug-eyed and said, "Is that the way you eat grits?"

As a Chicago boy I had heard of grits but had never seen them before. Now I had learned something and filed it away for future reference. But rather than exhibit my ignorance, I smiled self-assuredly and said, "Oh yes, this is how we eat grits in Chicago." He was amazed as I finished the bowl, which tasted terrible. But I kept my eye on him and discovered that the proper way to eat grits is with butter and salt and pepper.

Some days later I happened to be sitting at the same table with this same rangy mountaineer. Grits again were served that morning and under his watchful eye I took a bowl, scooped up some grits and again poured on milk and sugar. Somehow I managed to eat the mess.

The whole tragedy of the human predicament is demonstrated in this incident. We do not want to admit our mistakes. We would rather go to hell maintaining our innocence than to say, "I was wrong." Specific confession of sin seems to be extremely difficult for most of us in life's situations. Many in psychiatric work maintain that emotional and mental illness is often caused by our insistence that we are right. By admitting some error of long standing, we move toward maturity and healing. God asks us, "Do you want to be healed of some emotional or moral or physical ailment or do you want healing in some relationship?" When we can reply, "Yes. I have been wrong, I want to make things right and begin again," Jesus challenges us to take up our bed and walk. It may mean asking forgiveness or a change of jobs or to start fresh in any number of costly ways.

Another factor in man's predicament is his desperate need for love. This perhaps underlies our defensiveness and refusal to admit error. Being made in the image of God, we are not like God, but made to need God and His love. We are meant for love and have an almost unlimited need. It is so important for us to be loved by family and friends and colleagues that we dare not reveal our imperfections lest we be rejected. This is the motivation behind self-righteousness and pretense. It is this need for love that makes us destroy the very people for whom we care the most.

When we lived in Illinois, I owned a dog named Jock. He was a miserable dog who destroyed my wife's rugs and the neighbor's shrubs and the nocturnal peace of the neighborhood. But he had one outstanding quality. He loved me deeply.

As I went to the church or the hospital or made calls, Jock used to follow my car and always arrived shortly after I did, much out of breath. I would pretend to be angry when I saw him coming and would always sternly rebuke him. But inwardly I would gloat and think, *I'll bet few people have a dog that loves them as much as mine loves me.*

All this time my wife kept saying a prophetic word, as wives have a way of doing. She pointed out that if Jock wasn't chained, or trained to stay at home, he would surely be run over some day. Some day came. He was not only run over but killed and I was the one who killed him! He caught up to me at a stop sign and, not knowing he was there, I ran over him.

There is certainly truth in the old song, "You Always Hurt the One You Love." But it wasn't my love for Jock that destroyed him. It was my great need for his love. As parents we destroy our children because we need them so much that we act not in their best interests but out of our need. Jesus Christ offers to give us a new Spirit to motivate us and control us. This Spirit does not need people in this destructive way, but makes it possible for them to act on the basis of others' needs, rather than their own.

I cannot change the things in me that are most destructive. The question is: Am I willing to be changed? This is God's business. When we put ourselves into His hands, willing to be made new, we find that He is not only able but eager. Such is His love!

The Canadian college student mentioned earlier did go home to his family and was able to tell his parents that he loved them. This opened up a whole new relationship where they, with tears in their eyes, could express their love for him. Parents and a teen-ager discovered a new dimension of life and communication. It began when a son experienced God's love and received a new Spirit and a new ability to love.

Some years ago God confronted a redcap at Grand Central Station who hated his job and all the menial and degrading aspects of it. When Ralston Young, Redcap 42, heard Jesus Christ's challenge, "Dare to live now," he responded. He thought he would be given a new job, but found that God did not intend to change the circumstances of his life. Instead, God, through this redcap, has performed one of the most amazing ministries of our time. Three times a week at noon there is a prayer meeting on Track 13 which has attracted thousands over the years. Lives have been changed and re-directed, marriages healed, and problems solved. It began when one redcap accepted his environment and heredity and circum-stances and responded to God's challenge for healing and new-ness. This redcap, at the heart of New York City, has learned how to love others in a redemptive way.

A beautiful young mother in the middle of a nervous break-down was taken to a large hospital in St. Louis where she resisted all therapy. She was hurt that her husband and her mother would permit her to be confined to the psychiatric ward. For weeks she was sullen and morose and unco-operative.

One day she was standing by the barred windows of the ward looking out on Kings Highway which runs by the hos-pital. All of a sudden this woman, who had grown up in the church and knew the great truths about God, suddenly heard Him say to her, "Ruth, I love you. You don't have to live like this. Stop struggling and let me have your life and all of the resentments in you." When this awareness of God's love and Christ's presence came, something in her broke and she felt released. When she confided this to her doctor later that day, he told her that he saw an astonishing change. He called her husband and she was released the next day and went home to live a new life, with a new center and a new sense of her own worth.

God is trying to speak to us in all the circumstances of life. He wants to do more for us than merely relieve our pain or alter our circumstances or make life more comfortable. He is trying to show us the smallness of our own concerns and to demonstrate what His life in us can be if we give Him a chance.

Toward the end of World War II, in a Japanese concentration camp, the guards, learning of the imminent approach of the American army, unlocked the gates and fled to the woods. But the prisoners inside did not know this and remained in their cells. When the liberators came, they had only to announce to the prisoners that they were already free.

God has liberated all men through Jesus Christ. No one really has to be a prisoner of circumstances or environment. The good news is that we are *already free.* The message we announce to our friends is that freedom is available for all because of God's love and power in Jesus Christ. The only conditions seem to be that we admit we are prisoners and then risk leaving the security of old patterns and walk out into sunlight and freedom. It is not easy to live responsibly and in freedom and it is a challenge. Jesus says, "I came to bring release to the captives," and "I came that you might have life and have it abundantly." Dare to live now!

WHAT IS YOUR NAME?

2.

WHAT IS
YOUR NAME?

A New Name Can Make You a New Person

A COLLEGE STUDENT at a recent conference was asked, "What is the most meaningful thing that has happened to you recently?" His answer was surprising. "Let me tell you," he said. "Several weeks ago I had my handwriting analyzed and was told that I am an extrovert. I didn't know that. All my life I have been timid and shy, with a huge inferiority complex. But now that is all changed and I have been having a marvelous time these last few weeks!" And he wasn't fooling! A new name had given him the power to become a new person.

The Bible's story of Jacob and his twin brother Esau is as fascinating and contemporary as the children next door. Jacob was a mother's boy and his brother was an outdoorsman. Thus the seeds of life are sown!

The very name "Jacob" means "supplanter" or "cheat." Jacob cheated his brother. He cheated his father. He cheated his father-in-law. He lived up to his name. The turning point in his life came as he was leaving his father-in-law with two of

25

his daughters for wives and half of his livestock secured by trickery. As Jacob traveled toward home, he learned that his brother was coming to meet him with a large force of men.

Such a setting is perfect for conversion. Jacob is the man who has been "adjusting" his income tax when word comes that the Bureau of Internal Revenue wants to look at his books. He is the man who has been cheating on his wife and discovers that someone has told her. He is the student who has been putting off studying all semester and then comes to exam time. Life has a way of bringing us up short. One day we all face who we are and what we have done to people.

Suddenly Jacob faced a lifetime of deceit in the imminent approach of Esau. The night before he was to meet his brother, who had every right to rob him or thrash him or kill him, he was ready to hear what God had to say. He sent his family and servants and cattle on ahead and waited by the brook of Jabok. There he met God and wrestled with Him all night. As dawn came, the Person with whom he wrestled said, "Let me go, for the dawn is coming!" (One cannot see the face of God and live.)

But Jacob said, "I will not let You go unless You bless me."

Here is the really strange thing. When God said to Jacob, "I will bless you," God went on to ask, "What is your name?"

"My name is Jacob" (or cheat).

And God said, "Your name is no longer Jacob. It is Israel. Cheat, you have become a prince. That is your real name."

And the amazing thing was that this man became a prince of God, the person for whom the Israelite nation is named, and for whom Christians are named because we are the new Israel. He was the spiritual founder of all that we cherish, both as Jews and Christians, because God called him by his rightful name and he became what he was called.

We find this happening all through the Bible. When a man is ready for a blessing, God often gives him a new name – Simon became Peter, and Saul became Paul.

In subtle ways we give each other names-within-names. And the devastating thing is we become what we are called. Each of my children has a particular name and knows exactly what I mean when I call out, "Christine!" "Peter!" or "Mark!" All too often the name means that they must be more careful about their things, pick up their rooms, return library books, improve their table manners, study harder, bathe more often, or treat each other more lovingly.

How Do You See Yourself? Is your name Timid, or Dishonest, or Self-conscious, or Fearful, or Indifferent, or Reserved? The name by which God calls you might be just the opposite. It may be that your real name is Courageous, or Faithful, or Warm, or Generous.

About a year ago I met a man at a clergy retreat. At the opening meeting tempers got out of hand. Many of us were somewhat edgy and ruffled. This particular man, though not one of the official leaders, was the person who again and again was God's catalyst to change the atmosphere. His humor and insight and honesty were refreshing.

The next morning at breakfast he walked by my table. I grabbed his hand as he went by and said, "Trevor, I want you to know that I thank God for you."

"Oh, Bruce," he said smilingly, "I thank God for myself!"

I was amazed. I thought, this explains it. He can love others because he loves himself. He has all the troubles we have and is not perfect, but he can love himself because he knows that Jesus Christ loves him and he dares to call himself "Beloved."

How Do You See Others? If the names we call ourselves determine who we are, do the names we call others determine who they become? I have seen this happen and have marveled at it.

We had a thumb-sucker in our family who finally got to first grade and still sucked his thumb. I was frantic and tried everything I knew to break him of the habit, including scoldings, arguments, prayer with him, prayer for him, and the vile-tasting things that are concocted to put on children's thumbs to deter them from this persistent habit. But he was unable to stop. I kept telling him that I was doing all this for his own good and he heartily agreed!

But one day I realized what my true motives were. I was really embarrassed to have my child advertising to the world the emotional needs of his own home and the inadequacy of his parents. I saw that my love for this child was conditioned by my need for him to stop this habit. When God showed me this, I made a new commitment of myself to Him and began to affirm what a truly wonderful son I had.

I stopped correcting, nagging, or even referring to the thumb-sucking in any way. God had set me free and I secretly called my son by a new name, "Mr. Wonderful." I didn't care if he ever stopped sucking his thumb. The miracle is that in ten days he stopped cold and hasn't sucked his thumb since.

People often behave the way they do because of a name we force on them. An employer, an employee, a son, a daughter, a husband, or a wife can be put in a box by the name we give consciously or unconsciously. But I know firsthand how the miracle of a new name works, for I have been on the receiving end too.

Last summer our family had planned a long automobile trip across the United States and Mexico and I grew panicky as the departure date grew near. I am a compulsively neat, fussy, meticulous person who should never have inflicted himself on a wife and children. I want everything clean and in its proper place. For me things tend to become more important than people. Persons like me make it awfully hard for others and while God has done a great deal to set me free from this condition, I was afraid that a twelve-thousand-mile trip with five people and a Springer spaniel in one car would undo it all. I did not want to spoil the trip of a lifetime for my family.

On the third day of our trip, as we were having breakfast with friends in Montgomery, Alabama, I said to our gracious hostess, "Louise, you and Sid better pray for me these next two months so I won't be a block to God. I am a real neurotic, you know, and need a daily miracle."

Mark (our seven-year-old), who was sitting next to me, said, "Daddy, what's a neurotic?"

"He is a crabby old man."

"Oh, Daddy, you're not crabby!"

I was all set to tell him to cut the flattery, when I looked into his eyes and saw that he meant what he said. I was struck dumb. Was it true that this little boy did not see me as a crabby daddy?

We had an amazing trip and I had only one really bad time during those eight weeks. (That's not a bad average for a neurotic!) And I think the turning point came when my young son called me by a new name. He saw me through Christ's eyes and saw who I really am. I became the person I always wanted to be!

After I had preached in a New York church last year, a lovely young woman came up and said, "You know, Bruce, God has really changed my life since the conference two months ago. I have been having a terrible time with my mother for several years. She and I share an apartment and we fight all the time. She is possessive and demanding and we just go at it. I have prayed and prayed but nothing ever happened. But God worked a miracle at the last conference.

"The change came when Don James (Director of the Pittsburgh Experiment) told a story about two psychiatrists with offices in the same building. They often rode up on the same elevator together in the morning. The one who got off first invariably turned around and spat on his colleague. The other would calmly pull out his handkerchief and wipe his face, tie, and suit before getting off a few floors later.

"One morning the elevator operator could contain his curiosity no longer. As he was closing the door on the first psychiatrist, he said, 'For heaven's sake, Doctor, tell me why your colleague always does this to you.' The second psychiatrist calmly replied, 'Oh, I don't know. That's *his* problem!' "

The young woman told me that this story made her realize that her mother's behavior was her own problem. "God wants me to love her just the way she is and try to make life fun for her. I have changed tremendously since I saw this and God has even begun to change her!"

As long as we pray for people as problems, we will have problems on our hands. If we pray for a nagging mother, we will always have a nagging mother. If we pray for an indifferent husband, that is exactly what we will have. But claiming a new name for another may open the door for a miracle.

How Do You See Situations? Situations, too, become what we call them. We can pray for a problem office or a problem school or a problem home and forget the Lordship of Christ over every circumstance. We don't take Jesus Christ into our office, school, neighborhood, or church. He is there already. He wants us to discover Him there and claim the place for Him.

The first time the Israelites came out of Egypt heading for Canaan, their spies reported, "We can't take the place. It's full of giants, large armies, and walled cities." The Israelites believed the spies and doubted God's promise, so God made them wait forty years and raised up a whole new generation. Then new spies went in and reported on the same situation — the same walled cities and the same large armies, "We can take this place because God has said so. The land is ours!"

Now, do we see a problem business or a problem school or neighborhood like that? Do we pray, "Lord, this is Your business I'm working in. Nobody here may know it but You and me. I may be only a janitor (or a clerk or secretary or salesman), but this is Your business because the whole world is Yours. Lord, I belong to You, so I claim this place for You."

I know a man who some years ago was a junior executive in a business. He had begun his Christian life by facing up to some failures in his marriage and family. After God began to work in his life by changing these basic relationships, he began to face his job. In a small fellowship group that met weekly for study and prayer, he said one night, "You know, I can't stay in my job. I'm being asked by my superiors to do things that are dishonest. I'm low man on the totem pole and I can't fight it. But as a Christian I can't be dishonest."

We all prayed and for nine months he looked for a new job. He would have taken half the salary just to get out of that situation. But after months of closed doors, he finally said to the group, "I think I'm supposed to stay where I am and let God change the business through me." Two weeks later a young salesman who had been one of the most irreligious and immoral men in the business invited him to attend his baptism. God had changed his life and these two men became a team. Once a week over lunch they met to pray for the business and for each of the office staff by name. Soon there were three men meeting for lunch to claim God's best for the business.

Although not a word was said to anyone, within a year the ethics, philosophy, and moral fiber of the company were so changed that none of the three was asked to do a dishonest thing. It all began when one man said, "Lord, I claim this place for You." Incidentally, this man is now a senior executive and the primary person responsible for setting company policy.

As Christians we believe that God loves us and that Jesus Christ is alive and in the world working for our good. We believe that He has all power and that He wishes to transform us and make us and our world new. Finding your real name or the real name of others may be the beginning of this miracle.

ARE YOU FUN TO LIVE WITH?

3. ARE YOU FUN TO LIVE WITH?

The Acid Test

IN THE MIDDLE of our comfortable weekly luncheon meeting of Christian businessmen in midtown Manhattan, a Congregational minister from New England, Lee Whiston, dropped a bomb when he asked us, "Are you fun to live with?"

Most of the regular members of the group had from time to time confessed problems pertaining to their families. But with Lee's question, our traditional Christian concern for our families was shattered. Lee suggested that if we were living as Christ would have us, our families would enjoy living with us.

Well, we have never forgotten Lee's question, and each of us lives with it daily and refers to it in the group from time to time. God used that question to check my own motives and attitudes. Why do I want my wife or my children "to be more Christian" at times? Is it because I want God's best for them or because I want God to change some annoying trait in their lives that is creating a problem in mine? Is my motive really love — or am I using God to nag my family?

Several years ago when I had been having a faithful devotional time each morning (and my wife had not), I greeted her very irritably at the breakfast table. She had the Christian love to suggest that if this was all my "quiet time" was producing, maybe it would be better for me to spend the time in bed. Going to work on the bus that morning, I saw how I had been misusing that time in the morning, and was only feeding my self-righteousness. If I had really been spending time in God's presence, it would have made me a different person at the breakfast table.

The home is the most difficult — and rewarding — place for any Christian to put his faith to work. It's much easier to be effective and loving and faithful and gentle with people we only see from time to time. Unfortunately, we cannot fool the people who share our home. I am convinced that *we are what we are at home!*

Years ago I actually thought my family held me back spiritually. Now I see that God has given me at least one place where I can test how far I have come in this new life and relationship which He offers.

The home is the place where Christ can speak most clearly. I would rather hear God speak through almost anyone else than through my wife or my children. I can "take it" when He speaks through the minister, or through a friend, or through a book, or through His Word. But to recognize God speaking through my wife's loving rebuke or suggestion takes a great deal more grace. And if God is to speak clearly, whom can He better use than the one who sees me most clearly, loves me most unreservedly, and understands my needs most deeply?

At the heart of our Christian conviction is the belief that God wills newness of life, peace, joy, and love, not only for individuals, but for families. Here are four things we feel

God has been trying to show our family over the years, so that we can co-operate with His purpose and plan for us.

The first is the most difficult. *If you really want God to make your home new, you must let Him begin with you.* It is difficult for the member of the family, whether parent or child, who thinks he is "furthest along spiritually" to make the first move in a total surrender of his will and life to Christ. The instinctive thing is to hope that the others will catch up to us, so that we can "go all the way" together. This is never the case. One member of the family must be the spiritual pioneer and become totally vulnerable to the others in the family for Christ's sake to initiate God's action in a home.

I remember a couple who were married for nine years and who were living in hell. She claimed that he was romantically and emotionally cold and escaped from the home at every opportunity. She was involved in many civic and social and church organizations to find meaning for her life. Her husband, on the other hand, detested the kind of homemaking and cooking that his wife did (or rather did not do) and said that he could not feel warm toward someone who was so irresponsible in the home. Each declared that should the other change, he or she would follow suit.

One day the wife came to see me, on the verge of a divorce. I will never forget the miracle that began to happen when she promised God, on her knees, that she would be everything that her husband wanted her to be as a homemaker, for Christ's sake. She went home then, not out of a sense of duty but out of a new and deeper experience of God's love, and began to minister to her husband out of the fullness of that love. It took about a year for the husband to respond totally and to face up to the person God wanted to make of him as a husband.

Many of us live in a stalemate and cry, "Unfair! Unfair!" But the only way to break the stalemate is for one to go all the way. Each going halfway is never God's solution for a marriage.

There is an amazing verse in I Peter 3:1 that says, "You wives be submissive to your husbands so that some, though they do not obey the word, may be won without a word by the behavior of the wives." (That verse applies equally to husbands!) How wise the Apostle Peter was in sensing that we are not to talk about our faith at home, or if we do, to talk very sparingly. The thing that counts is to live a new and radiant life day by day and to be "fun to live with."

A second thing that our family must learn again and again is *how to love in God's way.* We are all aware of how children learn to manipulate their parents. They know how to "butter up" Father for an increase in allowance, the use of the car, or permission to do something usually forbidden. Unfortunately, most adults relate to each other in just the same way only with more sophistication.

When God's love captures us and we have the resources from within to live out the pattern for love described by the Apostle Paul in I Corinthians 13, we no longer have to manipulate people, but are free to be vulnerable to them and to their demands. This is what Christ meant in the great commandment to love one another as He has loved us. We have the promise that this kind of love never fails.

God's love working through us is permissive and unconditional. That means it is not conditioned by the response we get from people but by God's abundant supply in us. It offers freedom to others rather than rigidity. It is wrong to force family prayers or church attendance on an unwilling spouse or grown children. If Jesus Christ has truly made us new, we then have the resources to live so that they will *want* to pray and worship with us.

My wife and I laugh often at how we must continually learn to give love in terms meaningful to the other. Each of us would rather give love in the ways that we enjoy giving rather than in the ways the other enjoys receiving. How many hundreds of times in our fourteen years of marriage have I come home to a freshly baked pie. When God has spoken to her and convicted her of some failure in our relationship, she has often expressed her love or repentance by baking a pie. Now I don't especially like pie, but I have had to eat an awful lot of it in fourteen years!

In the same way, I have come home ready to hug and kiss and whisper sweet nothings to a spouse with whom I was most unloving or in violent disagreement a few hours earlier. At such times romance is the last thing that she wants from me!

We keep learning from God what to do after He has changed one of our hearts. We need to ask Him *how* to express this new love that we feel so that the other can receive it unmistakably. God wants to love people through us and He has to show us His unique strategy for loving each person He sends us.

One of my favorite contemporary theological works is the comic strip "Peanuts." Some months ago poor old Charlie Brown was coming home from a baseball game muttering, "One hundred and forty to nothing! . . . I just don't understand it! . . . And we were *so sincere!*" How often I have been sincere in expressing a new love God has given me for someone at home or in the office or elsewhere, but my strategy was all wrong. We need more than sincerity and a change of heart. We need to let the Holy Spirit show us how He can get through us in ways that will be meaningful to those on the receiving end.

I received a great deal of help a few years ago from a small group we belonged to in Illinois. One couple was concerned about a pre-school daughter, their only child. The father, who was extremely busy in all manner of church, civic, and scouting activities, felt that he was so out of touch with his daughter that he would have to drop some worthwhile activities and spend more time with her. He tried this with no result. One night he came to the group excited. He told us that God had revealed to him that it was not more time that his daughter needed but *all of him* for a brief time each day. He had been aware that when he was playing games with her or reading to her or doing anything with her he always had part of his mind on something else, or was carrying on a conversation with his wife, or was watching T.V. His daughter never had more than half of him. She reacted to this (as all of us do) and had all the symptoms of being unloved and rejected.

When God showed this man that one of the ways to love is to give another one's undivided attention, the relationship with his daughter took on a new dimension. This same thing is true for husbands and wives, brothers and sisters, roommates and all others with whom we are in contact. I will always be grateful for this lesson. I have had to learn it again in each new relationship.

The third lesson our family is learning has to do with *total honesty*. Real communication between God and man or between man and man requires total honesty. Most of us hide behind our masks and pretend to be people we are not. How hungry our family is to know us as we really are and to be known as they really are.

Our children need to know of our past failures and what we did when we were their age. They also need to know of our present failures and where we need forgiveness today. If in our family prayers we can be honest about ourselves, we do more to introduce our children to God than in all of our prayers for them. As a matter of fact, we must do much more praying with them. (It is best to pray *for* them in our private devotions.) In marriage we need to open our hearts totally to a spouse and learn to say, "I am sorry" or "I was wrong" at the appropriate times.

What happens when our children see us lose our tempers, become unfair or unjust, and then kneel in family prayers with them and pray for all the missionaries around the world and the minister in the church and Aunt Martha and Uncle Jim? They know this is phony and is not really being honest with God at all. When we can include prayers for our present needs in their presence (of which they are all too aware), they will almost invariably respond to the reality of Christ themselves.

The main thing to remember is never to hesitate being honest about yourself, but always hesitate being honest about another.

I believe that God will show us how to say things to others about their needs in those rare times that require it. One Christmas morning I received a handsomely wrapped package from my youngest son, which turned out to be a bottle of deodorant. On the card were the words, "Not because you do. So that you won't!" What tact! I have often wished that when it did seem right to talk to someone else in the family about his needs, I could have the gift to say things that way.

As we meet in prayer and discussion groups, we need to be

honest about some of the desperate situations we get into as families. I remember sitting at lunch with a group in Ontario who were talking about marriage. One of the women, a charming person of early middle years, was telling about her own past and present difficulties with a problem husband (the only kind God makes!). Someone asked, "Did you ever think of divorce?" She replied with a perfectly blank face, "Divorce? No! Murder? Yes!"

We all laughed and from that point the conversation took an entirely different turn. We began to be honest about the cost of being God's people and discovering newness as husbands and wives together. That kind of honesty in any Christian group is a gift.

The final thing that I personally struggle most with is *letting others in the family minister to me.* As a clergyman, I have an idea that I must always be right and the source of all Christian truth. Christ tries to show me that He is in my home independently of me and that some of His greatest truths come not only from my wife but from my children, even the youngest. God is there and He is working and I must enjoy being on the receiving end as others are used by Christ to minister to me. I believe that I am becoming free of having to bring Christ to my family. I might add that it is a great deal more fun to discover Him already here in our midst.

However, the battle is not easy. About a year ago I was having a difficult relationship with a wonderful Christian man. He seemed to judge me and criticize me no matter what I did. One day he wrote me a letter. I was furious and brought it home to my wife. "How in the world can I answer this?" I grumbled and showed it to her. She made several suggestions that I disposed of quickly because I didn't think she understood the devious nature of this man's spirit.

Finally she turned to me and said, "Why don't you take the advice you're so free to give all the rest of us?" (I knew something was coming!)

"What is that?" I asked.

"Why don't you admit to God that you have no love in your heart for this man and ask Him to change you?"

"That's ridiculous!" I shouted, and stomped out of the room to read the evening paper until dinner was ready.

That night in saying prayers with my ten-year-old daughter, I no sooner got to my knees than I had to face what I knew God had been trying to say to me through my wife. I asked His forgiveness in my daughter's presence and asked God to change me. My daughter concluded her prayers by saying, "Lord, you know that Father is a difficult man to change, and yet we know You can do it, and I ask You to give him Your love for this man."

Now this is not the role I have chosen for myself. I would rather be the teacher, the prophet, and the authority in my home. But frankly, this does not always work, and lately I've begun to enjoy being a learner with my family at the feet of Jesus Christ.

I have been told that traditionally there are two schools of thought in Germany. The industrial, practical, northern part of the country has this philosophy: "The situation is serious but not hopeless." In the southern part of Germany, more romantic and perhaps less practical, the philosophy seems to be: "The situation is hopeless but not serious."

The latter certainly expresses the basic Christian attitude about life. Apart from Christ's love and presence in us there is not much hope for us and our families, being the people we are. But when we take the Gospel seriously and realize that Christ is with us and contending for us, we can then look at the grimmest situation and say, "It's hopeless but not serious." Jesus Christ is alive and loves us and wants to give us and our families joy and love and newness of life!

LEARN TO LOVE

4. | LEARN TO LOVE

Life's Greatest Adventure

"LOVE IS THE MEDICINE for the sickness of the world," said Karl Menninger, one of the great contemporary figures in the field of medicine and psychiatry, some years ago.

Dr. Menninger told his staff, including doctors, nurses, orderlies, and cleaning people, that the most important thing they can offer a patient is love. For when people learn to give and receive love, they recover from most of their illnesses, whether physical or emotional. This is the secret behind the amazing success of the Menninger Clinic in Topeka, Kansas.

Other psychologists and psychiatrists are saying similar things. Erich Fromm believes that loneliness and the inability to love are the underlying causes of psychic and emotional disorders. Paul Tournier, the Swiss physician, talks of the need for persons to remove their masks and to discover and be discovered by other persons. Simple love and honest friendship can bring healing.

Hobart Mowrer, professor of clinical psychology at the

University of Illinois, denies the basic psychoanalytic theory that emotional illness results from a barrier between the conscious and the unconscious in a person. He believes emotional illness results from a barrier between the conscious self and other people. It is our inability to love and be loved, to have friends and be a friend in any depth, that causes much contemporary illness. When honesty and sharing of life begin, healing often begins.

Carl Rogers, founder of the famous nondirective school of counselling, says of persons that come to his University of Chicago school for training as psychotherapists that he can quickly train those who have what he apologetically calls "love." (He says there is no other word to describe the quality which makes a good counselor.) Without "love" no amount of training can make a man or a woman effective. And so the evidence mounts in medicine and psychology regarding the therapeutic need for love.

Moving to the political scene, many prophetic voices in government have spoken of the need for genuine love in America's foreign policy. This view has been wonderfully illustrated in the excellent book, *The Ugly American*, by Lederer and Burdick, which maintains that no give-away programs of material will really do the job in the world. The primary need is for love in the hearts of people who go out and administer our foreign policy. Our overseas ambassadors, whether for the State Department, the Peace Corps, or representatives of industry, must become rightly motivated. People respond to genuine love in other people — and to the lack of it.

While the underprivileged nations' most pressing needs are material and technical, their greatest need, as ours, is still for human love.

I recently spoke to a Swedish pastor who was visiting New

York. I asked him for the cause of the numerous teen-age gang riots in Sweden. He said that Sweden has achieved an almost perfect form of socialism where all material needs are effectively being met, but that the nation has forgotten how to help young people find a reason for living, a spiritual focus for life, and depth relationships. People still need more than medical care, material security, and peace to live life together successfully and creatively as individuals, families, or nations.

The communists are succeeding in winning neutral nations where we are failing, not because they genuinely love these nations but because they at least give the *appearance* of love. America, on the other hand, is like the rich uncle who enjoys giving gifts but not giving himself.

A veteran leader in foreign missions for the Presbyterian Church told me that when President Eisenhower visited Kabul, Afghanistan, not one of the 250 people in the American Embassy could translate the President's speech to the people. On the other hand, each one of the eighty employees of the Russian Embassy, including the chauffeurs, was able to speak the language. This gives some indication of the tragic lack of identification which has so often characterized our foreign affairs. We can be thankful that we are learning from our mistakes.

In other corners of the human arena the same plea is heard. There is a desperate suppressed cry for love coming from the works of the successful novelists and playwrights of Europe and America. Whether we read Albert Camus, Tennessee Williams, Françoise Sagan, or a host of others, or analyze many of the current plays and films, we are overwhelmed with the recurrent theme of loneliness and separation.

Our world is becoming increasingly aware of the need for love, both on the international scene and in the back wards of mental hospitals. Christ is calling His Church in this age to love people with His love in all the common affairs of daily life.

What is this love that the world is looking for? Christians know that God is love. Love is not a technique that can be learned; it is a gift. Erich Fromm says that when we need someone it is impossible truly to love him. He defines mature love as, "I love you, therefore I need you," rather than "I need you, therefore I love you." There is a profound difference. God needs us because He loves us, and when His love enters into us through Jesus Christ, we need people because we love them. The person who has not experienced this love of God must of necessity love others only because he needs them. Then true love is impossible.

Love does not have to prove itself. Much of our service to others in life comes because of an awareness that we do not love a person as we should and therefore must prove our love to him and to ourselves. This is why over-generous and non-disciplining parents betray the fact that they do not love their children enough. I know of one couple who insisted on taking an old father into their home when he would have been much better off in a place where he could have received nursing care and quiet. They had to prove to themselves and to him how much they loved him. When they finally saw how little real love they had for him, and prayed for a new kind of love, they were able to release the old gentleman to a different kind of life where both he and they were much happier.

Basically we know when we are loved with a divine love. When someone comes into our life filled with Christ's love, we respond to the divine in him. I know a woman who discovered this new way of love. She was on the visitation committee in her Episcopal church and brought altar flowers to shut-ins. One gruff old parishioner at the hospital said to his minister, "Tell that girl who was here Sunday that she can keep her blasted flowers but to come back. Something happened to me while she was here." This love is so different from anything the world knows that we never have to wonder if we are giving or receiving it.

Love is God's greatest weapon. When a living Christ can enter a human life and begin to act and move through it, everything changes. Two or three high-school students in one large city carried on a quiet war of love against a harsh, unfair, irritable teacher. Instead of reacting to her, which would have been natural, they began quietly to love her and secretly to pray for her in the classroom. She was in time transformed, and the entire class and school felt the impact. Illustrations could be given from every kind of life situation regarding the power of love to transform people and relationships.

How can Christians learn to love this way? Four basic principles can help us. The first two have to do with receiving Christ's love; the second two with transmitting His love to others.

First we must believe Christ loves us *just as we are*. We are impatient, grumpy, irritable, nagging, fault-finding at home or in the office or in school because we really hate ourselves. It is difficult to believe that right now, in the light of what we have just done, God loves us as much as He says He does. When I find myself critical of people I live with at home or work, I don't need more patience but time alone to let God remind me of His love for me. When I know that I am loved by Him and am forgiven for present failures, then I find the things that have been so irritating in my family members or colleagues become trivial. We must learn to take the Cross seriously and experience day by day and moment by moment

Christ's overpowering love and forgiveness, not only for sins past, but for sins present. He does not say to us, "Change, that I might love you." As we read the Biblical record of Jesus talking with people, we sense His total love for them as they are. This love motivates them to change. We do not repent *in order* to be loved, but *because* we are loved by Him.

Secondly, we must be ourselves at all times. "If the Son shall make you free, you shall be free indeed." We must not repress feelings that are wrong but let them come out where God can deal with them. We tend to think that being a Christian is to pretend love for those whom we do not love and smile meekly to hide the churnings inside. "Telling somebody off" may not be the Christian way, but it is certainly healthier than pretending nothing is wrong.

We Christians have a wonderful promise, "For there is therefore now no condemnation for those who are in Christ Jesus. . . ." We must be ourselves, believing that Christ loves us as we are and does not condemn us. "If we confess our sins, He is faithful and just to forgive us our sins. . . ."

In transmitting this love to others, the first principle is to let *others* be themselves. We must learn that it is not our job to change other people. Our job is to love them or to let God change us so that we *can* love them.

One of the most amazing centers of Christian love I know is Hidden Springs in Brantford, Ontario. Here a group of Christians are helping people adjust to life. One of the questions they keep asking their patients is, "Do you want to be right or do you want to be well?" When we stop having to prove to ourselves and to others that we are right, we have come a great way in learning how to transmit love.

We must learn not to take people at face value. We have to go beyond their faces to their hearts. Many people who

smilingly tell us that they are, "Fine! Fine!" are crying inside and are desperately lonely and confused, looking for
someone in whom to confide. If we can be sensitive to people,
we give them a chance to be themselves with us. If we can let
them know we understand something of disappointment and
sorrow and guilt, perhaps they can then tell us of their real
feelings and of the "impossible" turn life may have just taken.

Secondly, we channel the love of Christ to others by believing in Christ's love for every person we meet. Perhaps
this is the most revolutionary principle of all. Christ does
not ask us to feel loving toward everyone we meet. This is
impossible when someone has offended us or wounded us or
done something unfair or dishonest. But we can believe that
He loves that person at the very moment we are seething with
resentment. We are asked to use our wills to let go of our
resentment and to allow His love to come through us. It
doesn't matter how we feel about that person as long as we
are willing to be a channel of God's love to him. This is an
entirely different thing from trying to generate love or trying
to change our feelings. We must learn to live above the level
of feelings. By faith we can be a link between Christ and the
person in need.

Frank Laubach has provided many with perhaps the most
concrete way of opening the channel. He suggests that we
throw one arm up vertically to receive Christ's love and throw
the other arm out horizontally to channel it. We receive
Christ's love with one arm and aim it with the other.

If we are in a situation where this is physically impossible,
we can do this, "one arm up and one arm out," mentally. Over
and over again I have seen God not only change my feelings
in a moment but actually transform the person to whom I
have been a channel.

The greatest adventure in life is to experience the love of God in Jesus Christ and to transmit it to others. As Christians we must be clear about what this involves in every situation, to fulfill the mission that He has given us, "This I command you, to love one another as I have loved you."

PERSON TO PERSON

5. | PERSON TO PERSON

The Secret of Effective Communication

I HAVE A FRIEND who is extremely self-conscious. When he comes into a room where there are small children, he tries to ignore them, hiding behind a newspaper or book, or becoming absorbed in television. But invariably the children, whether they are his relatives or total strangers, climb all over him and refuse to leave him alone, even though he says, "Go away and stop bothering me." Children are not put off by his gruff exterior. They know that it hides a warm and genuine love.

On the other hand, these same children will sometimes run from a sweet old lady who says, "Come here, Dear, and give Auntie a big kiss." They know that inside she is no lover of little children and possibly no lover of anyone but herself.

People respond more to how we feel about them than to what we say to them. For years Dr. John Casteel has been saying to students at Union Theological Seminary in New York that dynamic Christian truth is transmitted *relationally* rather than *propositionally*, though he concedes that it is often a difficult truth for seminary students to comprehend, since their focus is so much on the theological content of the Bible.

Because I am fascinated by the way life-changing truth is communicated from person to person, I have recently been conducting an experiment. I have asked literally hundreds of people, in small groups and individually, two questions. The first is, "What single person has had the greatest influence on your life?" The replies have always been illuminating, both to me and to the people who have answered the question. Very few have pointed to such obvious people as parents or ministers. The persons most often mentioned are grade-school teachers or high-school teachers, older friends, distant relatives (frequently a grandparent), or a much older neighbor or Sunday school teacher.

The second question has been even more illuminating. I have asked them to describe the nature of their relationship with this person. Here are some of the significant characteristics of these dynamic relationships.

Identification. "The person who most influenced me treated me as an equal," is often said. The person was in some superior role, either because of age or experience or status. The important thing was that he did not use that superior position as a platform from which to help, but was able to stand alongside the other. Remember how Jesus washed the feet of the disciples and told us to do the same! D. T. Niles, of Ceylon, says that the Christian Church often misses the mark because we Christians would rather *give a service than be a servant.* The servant identifies with the person he is serving and is willing to be a subordinate. There is a vast difference between this and bringing another a service he needs, whether it be food, medicine, teaching, or counseling!

A few months ago a woman told several of us about a prayer and study group she had organized in her suburban neighborhood. For months this lovely woman had tried to help the "lost" in her neighborhood, but with little success. The group seemed hopeless. One morning she had a rare fight with her husband and the group was to meet that afternoon. At first she thought she would have to stay away. When she finally went, she broke down and told of what had happened, and concluded by saying, "I have no right to teach you. I shouldn't even be here in this condition!" Then guilt overwhelmed her and she left hurriedly. She was afraid that she had completely lost her effectiveness, only to find later that three of the young housewives made tremendous spiritual advances that day because their teacher had demonstrated that she was "one of them." If she was really like them *in their needs*, they concluded, they wanted to know her Lord!

Listening. "He was always interested in hearing about my problems and my ideas," is another description of this influential friend. We mistakenly think that our knowledge or insight is the greatest gift we can give to others. Often we bring them much further when we eagerly listen to what they are trying to say about themselves and their problems. We affirm their worth and dignity by taking them seriously.

It is illuminating to study Jesus' way with individuals. He often got a "case history." Jesus would draw out the demon-possessed, or those sick or in trouble, by asking the person what he understood of his own problem. The Holy Spirit may do more to convict a person out of his own mouth by what he says to a loving listener than by all of the good advice and insight that may come from the mouth of another.

Personal Honesty. "He let me know what his own problems and needs were," is another description I often hear. One hears a great deal of concern expressed that religion can become "too personal." But Jesus did not practice secrecy about Himself. The only way we could know about His temptations in the wilderness is that He must have told His disciples, for no one else was there with Him.

Paul Tournier, the eminent Swiss physician, has contributed much to the field of counseling and psychotherapy along this line. Dr. Tournier is successful because he is honest about himself with his patients and does not relate merely as a professional person to a client. He relates as a person to a person. It is amazing how God uses this to build therapeutic relationships.

One evening as a men's group was meeting in our office in New York, a man came in whom no one knew. Each thought that he had been referred by someone else in the circle, and so it was suggested he pull up a chair and join the six or eight men who were meeting for fellowship and prayer. He sat and listened as several individuals talked about present struggles toward becoming whole people and effective Christians.

Finally the leader turned to the stranger and asked who he was. "My name is Paul," he said, "and as long as you have been honest, I will be honest too. I am a dope addict. I came here to rob this office to get a fix, but I think I have found something better." Paul stayed to pray and asked God for help with his serious problem simply because he heard some other men being honest.

Vulnerability. "He trusted me" is another answer I often hear. We need to trust others in costly ways even as Jesus trusted Judas, not only with His money but with His reputation and His life. This is one of Jesus' supreme messages for us and He commands us to love one another as He has loved us.

The night before this chapter was written, my wife and I

had dinner with a young couple who have in recent years discovered the reality of Jesus Christ. For some time we have known of their "experiment of faith." The wife began first by making a personal moral inventory and then praying with another person. Her three biggest problems had been her relationship to a daughter who was severely handicapped, a frustrated ambition to be a professional singer, and a husband who was fast becoming an alcoholic.

The morning after this prayer her husband woke up with a dreadful hangover. Without saying a word of reproach, his wife began to rub his back. He describes this startling change in her, which is still going on, as the incident that finally brought him to a surrender of his own life to Jesus Christ some months later.

To lay one's life down for another while he is confused and rebellious is hardly possible apart from the presence of God. How afraid we are that the other will take advantage of us if we don't preach to him and moralize with him about his problems. I recently had an effective Christian tell me that one of the secrets of his life is, "Never let another person's sins bother you until they bother him." If we really live this out, we will become involved with people in a costly way.

Willingness To Receive. "This person would often ask me to help him or pray for him," is another frequent answer. Jesus frequently initiated a new relationship by asking for help. He was never reluctant to ask for food or lodging or water or even company in His loneliness and temptation. This was His first step in graciously opening other lives for the help they needed from Him. We need to discover how to receive help from others, so that they may then accept what God may want to give them through us. As one friend of mine often says, "Don't be a stingy receiver."

Several years ago, I became suddenly ill at a conference in Bloomington, Illinois. I had all the usual symptoms that go with the flu, including chills and fever. I took to my bed in the men's dormitory. Within the space of one hour, six different people heard about my need and came to offer help. One anointed me with oil for healing — my first experience of it! Another knelt and offered prayer. The third person was a woman doctor who came in and gave me some aspirin, took my pulse, and reassured me that, in all probability, I had a twenty-four-hour flu bug. The fourth person brought me a tray of food, which was the last thing in the world I wanted at that time! The fifth just expressed concern, while the sixth, a wonderful Finnish masseuse, came in and sang hymns in Finnish while she gave me a massage.

Two things happened. First, I was healed within the hour. I don't know which one of those people was the channel of God's healing, but I suspect they all were used. But second, and even more exciting, I became aware that God was trying to teach me how important it is to receive help from Him through others. It is much easier for me to give than to receive, which has often been a block in relationships. I still thank God for that lesson and am grateful for my six "teachers."

So God communicates His life through us to others. The apostolic succession of New Life from person to person is a twentieth century reality unbroken since Pentecost.

YOU AND YOUR JOB

6. YOU AND YOUR JOB

Bringing Your Faith to Work

HOW DO YOU SEE YOUR JOB? Whether you are a homemaker, a student, or a factory worker, the attitude you have about your work reveals a great deal about your faith. The Bible indicates that every Christian ought to feel a sense of vocation in his work. If you are miserable or bored in your work, or dread going to it, then God is speaking to you. He either wants to change the job you are in or — more likely — He wants to change *you*.

Remember the story about the blind man whom Jesus healed? After our Lord touched his eyes, He asked the man what he saw. He reported that he saw "men as trees walking." When he had received a second touch from the Master, he saw men clearly. I suspect that many of us need a "second touch" by Christ to see our jobs in their right perspective.

A friend in Illinois had joined a small group of seekers meeting for prayer and Bible study and the sharing of their faith each week. Although he had come a long way in his Christian commitment, each week he complained about the customers in his store — how unfair they were, how demanding, and how they took advantage of him.

But one day this man received a "second touch" by God and began to see the people who came into his store, whether to buy a package of nails or a washing machine, as people sent by God. He anticipated each sale as an adventure in personal relationships.

At Christmas time, with all the rush of increased sales, this man said to the group one night in amazement, "You know, what surprises me is how the people in this town have changed. Last Christmas they were rude, pushy, and demanding, but this year I haven't had a difficult customer in my store! Everyone is understanding and trying his best to co-operate." They all laughed. They knew the change had not been in the town but in the storekeeper.

But in a more profound way, perhaps the change was also in the town. As we see people through the eyes of faith, they actually do change. They respond to us almost directly in proportion to the amount of love we have for them as people.

Let me suggest five questions each of us should periodically ask ourselves about our job.

(1) *Why am I here in this job?* Do you feel you are in your present job because of an accident? Because you happened to answer an ad, or your brother-in-law got tired of having you sit around and found you a job? Because of ambition? These attitudes certainly undercut any sense of Christion vocation. We should feel we are in our work because God has called us to it, in just as real a way as He has called any bishop, clergyman, or priest.

Several months ago a man asked me to call on him in his large office in New York City. He said, "A year ago I turned my life over to Jesus Christ. It happened in my church." He then described the change that had begun to happen in his home — new communication between him and his wife; deeper understanding of his teen-age daughter. There were many other evidences of his new commitment.

Then he said, "I find now, a year later, that I am still behind the same desk doing the same job in the same way, and I suspect something is wrong. If Christ has come in as Lord of my life, things ought to be very different in what I do eight or ten hours a day." He was right, of course. Now he is exploring, along with some other men, the opportunities and strategy for Christian ministry in daily work.

We must dispense with the myth that commitment to Christ means becoming a clergyman or that work done inside a church building or in a church organization is more holy, somehow, than work done in the market place. Christ came to give us a sense of calling in everyday work. This is where the world is changed, and where the Kingdom is built.

Jesus Himself was a working man, and He called twelve working men to be His initial disciples. He could have been born into a priestly family, but He was not. We must understand the really radical thing God has done in Jesus Christ, in wanting to build a new world and a new Kingdom primarily through committed working men.

(2) *For whom am I working?* Are you working for God, or for men? You cannot really serve both. When we are addicted to people's praise and thanks and rewards, we are in a real way under the tyranny of men and are working for them.

Often I feel terribly sorry for the wives and mothers in the world who work such long hours and never seem to be finished with their chores. If they are working for the appreciation and thanks of their families, they seldom or never get it. But when we work for God, we are free to serve others no matter how unreasonable or thankless they may be. Our reward is God Himself saying to us, "Well done, good and faithful servant."

Daily chores take on new meaning when we work for God rather than men. One woman has this inscription over her kitchen sink: "Divine services held here three times daily." What a marvelous freedom in washing greasy pots and pans, not for those who eat from them, but for a Lord who puts a woman into a home to serve a family for Him!

We need continually to ask ourselves whether we are willing to risk our jobs and our financial security in obedience to Jesus Christ. When we really work for God, and know that it is He to whom we are responsible, and from whom we get our reward, we are then free to be His people in any given situation.

(3) *What am I working for?* Wages? Prestige? Or am I working to do the will of God? This has much to say about our motives.

Christ's own life gives us a key. When He found people abusing others in the temple, He came in and violently upset the status quo. But when people wished to destroy *Him*, He let them drive nails into His hands. Perhaps this is the kind of freedom Christian men and women need in their jobs; not to protect their own interests, but to look to the interests of others; to protest when innocent people are being hurt, but not to protest for self-preservation. This freedom comes only when we can answer the question, "What am I working for?" with "To do the will of God."

Where is your security? Is it in the person who pays your salary or do you see him only as an agent whom God at this time has chosen to supply your needs? You cannot really love your boss or paymaster until you see him as God's agent. If you see him as your provider, then you cannot be honest with him, and fear and resentment are bound to color your relationship.

I have a wonderful Chinese friend, Moses Chow. His father was one of two sons in a family in pre-communist China. He had become a Christian and was told by his father that if he persisted in following this "new god," he would be disinherited.

There was wealth in the family, but Moses' father could choose only where he had found life, and life abundant. So, in his determination to follow Jesus Christ, he was disinherited and left China.

Moses Chow told us that his father went on to make a new home in a new country in the Far East, and has been quite successful as a Christian businessman. He left the security of the world and trusted God, who was able to provide. Meanwhile, Moses' grandfather and others fell victim to communism and lost everything. We don't follow God *because* He makes us secure, but our security is in God — even in economic matters.

(4) *With whom am I working?* God wants us always to be aware of the people next to us. It's not enough just to work honestly and industriously, for Christ calls us to be a priesthood of believers who willingly take responsibility for those who are our neighbors.

A railroad engineer came to his minister and asked to be put to work as a new Christian. The minister told the engineer that there was no position in the church open at the present time, but that there was a job, and it involved the question, "Is your fireman a Christian?"

This is the concept of the priesthood of believers, when we see that our primary job is not to be an elder, deacon, or vestryman in the church, but to be a priest to the man next to us in our daily work. This is where we need to recapture the marvelous vision God has for the priesthood of the laity.

God calls the laity to do a job the clergy cannot do in many instances. In a parish I once served, a close friend who was a doctor became quite ill. Though I visited him almost daily, I saw no improvement and no benefit from my visits. One day I went to see this Christian doctor and found him greatly improved and free from fear.

I asked him what had happened, and he told me of a visit he had had a few hours before from one of the senior surgeons in the area who had prayed with him and given him a prescription. The prescription was to read Joshua 1:9. My friend had been visibly touched by God, and not through a clergyman but through a brother physician.

(5) *What kind of place am I in?* Jesus Christ, by His very call to accept Him as Lord and Saviour, has brought us inside a revolutionary movement, so that the place we are in assumes tremendous importance.

No job is too menial to be of importance to a communist! Shouldn't this same thing be true for any Christian trying to build a worldwide Kingdom? Even a chambermaid making beds in a hotel can influence guests who go out and make decisions of worldwide importance. Christians should ask God to show them the nature of the place they are in. How important is the particular store, shop, industry, or service which is theirs? What could God do through that particular organization to change His world?

Recently I was speaking with a Congregational minister in New England. He told me of meeting with a group of high school students who wanted to know how to live their faith more effectively. He asked them to think hypothetically what they would do in their school if they were communists.

They brainstormed for a time and came up with a number of things they could do to sabotage the school: cut classes, sow discord, obstruct education in all kinds of ways, from telling lies to smoking in the basement.

Suddenly, one of the boys said, "Wait a minute, isn't this just what we are doing now!" It was a wonderful eye-opener for these young people to begin to see their high school as a place where Christ could begin to change the world through them. Later on they began to discuss just what it meant to be Christ's people, building a Kingdom in their own school.

There is a revolution going on in the world. Jesus Christ Himself is the leader, and when we accept Him as our Lord, He calls us into it with Him. He needs us. He wants us to see our jobs with the eyes of faith and understanding as something far more than a means of earning a livelihood. Our jobs are places where, as revolutionaries, we help to accomplish His revolution in the hearts and lives of men everywhere.

DISCOVERING A
CHRISTIAN MARRIAGE

7. DISCOVERING A CHRISTIAN MARRIAGE

Seven Words Unlock the Door

A FINE YOUNG ENGINEER I know, in the process of discovering a Christian marriage, said, "Marriage is wonderful, but it doesn't solve any of your problems." It is not supposed to! If you are unhappy before you marry, you will certainly be unhappy after you marry. Two people combine their problems when they marry, and living becomes even more complicated.

Christians believe that God intends marriage to be a wonderful, satisfying, and joyful relationship and that He has the power to make it so. And yet a truly happy marriage is not a common thing. Most of the marriages that fail never reach the divorce court.

We are surprised when a marriage "suddenly" breaks down. We are like the middle-aged man who began to lose his hair. Finally he had only one hair left on his head. He faithfully oiled and massaged that single hair. One morning he got out of bed and there on the pillow lay his one hair. With great anguish he cried out, "Great Scott. I'm bald!"

Marriage does not fail because one of the partners suddenly finds someone else who is more interesting. It is *because* the marriage relationship had already broken down that one of the partners began to look elsewhere.

No change in our circumstances is going to solve the basic problem in our marriage. A better house, more money, moving away from the "in-laws," or being able to have children will not really change a thing. We must become aware of the underlying causes of unhappiness that drive our partners to infidelity or alcohol or any of a hundred kinds of escape.

What is a Christian marriage? Basically it means that I can no longer do as I please. In too many marriages one or both partners do just exactly as they please and wonder why things aren't better.

This self-will can take many forms. It can be expressed as hostility. We resort to nagging or irritability or actual fighting with our spouse. Being afraid to face the genuine cause of a failing marriage, we choose certain areas for battle. We fight about where to squeeze the toothpaste tube, how to discipline the children, who spends the most money foolishly, why the house is not better kept, and whose habits make them "just like" their mother. Such fights give us a chance to express our hostility without getting into the deeper and more painful issues.

It ought to be said at this point that, when there is open hostility, we can assume there is still caring. The situation is more serious when a husband or wife does not even care enough to fight or get angry, and instead says, "You go your way and I'll go mine." In such a marriage a man recently told me that his wife seemed more like a college roommate.

When God is allowed into the lives of one or both of the people in a marriage, we see that the cause of unhappiness is within the individual. It is the feeling that we are not appreciated enough, that we give more love than we receive.

I talked with a couple recently about their marriage. The wife said, "But I always give in. I wish just once *he* would give in. If he loved me as much as I love him, *he would*." This is the basic frustration in all unhappy marriages.

It has been said that when two people marry, they become one, but the question often is, which one? Visualize two solar systems trying to occupy the same space at the same time; two suns vying for center with planets orbiting around each. The result would be chaos and collision. The same is true of a home with conflicting centers and different interests whirling around each. In some homes such a situation is solved by everyone yielding center place to one. Then the home centers around the mother or father or a child. Peace reigns, but the price is frustration and humiliation. This kind of peace is not the Christian answer.

In Christian marriage Christ is the center, and husband, wife, and children can find their proper orbit around Him.

Let us express this mathematically. In a marriage without Jesus Christ, 1 plus 1 equals 2. Where there are children, 1 plus 1 plus 1 plus 1 equals 4, and four centers in a home are hell!

The Bible says about marriage, "These two shall become one." Mathematically this means that 1 plus 1 equals 1. This sounds ridiculous in the science of mathematics, but it makes wonderful sense in the metaphysics of matrimony!

One attractive young couple came to realize that their budget was their biggest problem. Each felt that their tight budget and growing debts were the result of the other's irresponsibility and poor management. The subject was explosive and neither dared bring it up knowing the violent consequences. The wife expressed her rebellion by going on a periodic clothes buying spree, while the husband bought model trains.

When they admitted as new Christians that Christ could help them decide how they should spend their income, they were able in a short time to discuss their finances without anger, live within their income, and slowly begin to come out of debt. They set a time each week to go over the budget, and to remind them who had the final word, they always placed an empty chair at the head of the table.

Human love presupposes marriage to one's ideal. As disillusionment comes, the marriage breaks down. Christian love is not blind, but it has its eyes wide open. It does not vanish when the other's faults appear. A Christian marriage involves seeing and understanding the other person as he really is and loving him just that way.

Christ's plan for two people who are married and who live their lives in Him is that the wonderful glow of the courtship and honeymoon will not only last but deepen. True romance may not begin until we find this plan.

I can think of a couple married thirty years who are discovering Christian marriage after a lifetime of bickering and fighting. Today they are living in the glow of what it means truly to love each other. They are grandparents and also have young children of their own who share this new love in the home.

It all began with a conversation in which the wife expressed her life-long complaint. Her husband was hard to live with and touchy. He sulked and was unreasonable. He was extremely stubborn. Above all, *she* was active in her church and her husband was not. She wanted to know how to make her husband a Christian!

It was pointed out that if she were really a Christian, her only obligation was to make her husband happy, not good. This was a new thought. She saw that in spite of all of her church work, perhaps she had never let Jesus Christ become the center in her life.

One day she made a list of all the things she knew should be different in her life. Then she prayed, asking God to come into her life and change all these things. She discovered a wonderful new peace.

Five days later her husband, amazed by the wonderful change that had come over his wife, asked if the same thing could happen to him. He honestly faced the things that were wrong in his life and he prayed, asking Christ to forgive him and to change him and to take over his life. The marriage was transformed.

There is no way for God to change a marriage and leave the people involved unchanged. C. S. Lewis has said, "No clever arrangement of bad eggs ever made a good omelet." We waste too many of our prayers praying for the other person to change, when some really honest prayer for ourselves may do wonders.

Not long ago a woman came to her minister, begging him to tell her what to do with her alcoholic husband. She had taken all the abuse and humiliation and poverty she felt she could stand as the result of his drinking. Her minister asked her what she had done to try to change him. She said she had begged him, argued with him, shamed him, preached at him, read the Bible to him, threatened him, and prayed for him for years.

"Have any of these seemed to work?" the minister asked.

"No!" said the woman. "They have not."

"There is one thing you haven't tried. Why don't you pray

for *yourself*, instead of your husband, and ask God to change all the things in your life that you know are wrong?"

The woman tried it and it worked. Her husband stopped drinking. He no longer had to escape.

Anyone can discover a Christian marriage who will sincerely pray the prayer, "Lord, change this marriage beginning with *me*."

PRIMING THE PUMP

8. PRIMING THE PUMP

Three Essentials of a Life of Faith

THE FOLLOWING LETTER was found in a baking powder can wired to the handle of an old pump that offered the only hope of drinking water on a very long and seldom-used trail across the Amargosa Desert:

"This pump is all right as of June 1932. I put a new sucker washer into it and it ought to last five years. But the washer dries out and the pump has got to be primed. Under the white rock I buried a bottle of water, out of the sun and cork end up. There's enough water in it to prime the pump, but not if you drink some first. Pour about one fourth and let her soak to wet the leather. Then pour in the rest medium fast and pump like crazy. You'll git water. The well has never run dry. Have faith. When you git watered up, fill the bottle and put it back like you found it for the next feller.

(signed) Desert Pete

"P.S. Don't go drinking up the water first. Prime the pump with it and you'll git all you can hold."

Nowhere have I seen the principles of faith more clearly set forth. What a person would do coming along that trail, half dead from lack of water and with an empty canteen would reveal much about his faith. Faith is not so much an academic subject for discussion or a theological term from the Bible, as it is something on which our very life hinges.

Faith is composed of three ingredients. First, there must be an object. It is impossible just "to have faith." If you were a lonely traveler coming down that parched desert trail, you would have to trust in an unknown person named Desert Pete to keep from drinking the bottle of buried water. This would not be easy. He is a person you do not know. There is a great deal of evidence he is telling the truth, but there is no guarantee that he is not a practical joker or a lunatic. So, the first ingredient of faith is trust in someone or something, based on evidence but not infallible proof.

The second ingredient is risk. Faith is always costly. If you were walking down that trail without water, there would be nothing more precious to you in all the world than a bottle of water. Desert Pete tells you that if you drink any part of that bottle of water he has left, you won't get any from the pump. So, it is necessary to risk the very stuff on which your life may depend to get a safe and sufficient amount. Faith is always expensive.

The third ingredient is work. Some people have mistakenly interpreted faith as a substitute for work. Faith is not laziness. Desert Pete reminds us that after we trust and risk, we have to pump hard!

Everyone uses faith daily. You have to trust either a partner in marriage or in business. Sometimes that trust is misplaced. In business, money and reputation are risked; in marriage, your whole life. For success, both a business and a marriage require a tremendous amount of work and consecration by both parties.

So much for faith. But what about Christian faith? This is no different in its ingredients. First of all, one has to have faith in God and especially in the way God has revealed Himself to man in the person of Jesus Christ. It is not faith in a principle but faith in a person — the Person!

Second there is commitment that involves risk. A total commitment always has specific and immediate implications that involve risk. It may mean asking forgiveness of another, making a specific restitution, beginning to tithe, or changing jobs. The more we commit of ourselves to God in very specific terms, the better we can know Him and His plan for our lives.

Third, there is hard work. After one has had faith in God and committed his life to Him, then comes the hard work. Some people have interpreted the Christian faith as just a matter of hard work. This leads to a kind of living which may be religious, but is not necessarily Christian. Christian faith is more than hard work for Christ and His Kingdom. But I have never known an effective Christian who was lazy.

In the Bible, Abraham has been called the Father of the Faithful. Because of his faith in God he left his home in Ur of the Chaldees. By faith he gave up the known and the familiar for the unknown and unfamiliar. He committed his life and his family and all of his possessions to the leadership of God, who called him to a new life in a new land. To find that new land and the new life required years of hard work. All of the men and women of faith in the Bible have had similar experiences.

How do we practice Christian faith today? The rules are the same. First we must believe that God is. Then we must listen to Him. When God speaks, we must obey every order we get, and it usually requires a great deal of faith and hard work. If we trust Him, God will do for us those things we cannot do for ourselves. But he will not do for us those things that we can do!

Many people wonder how they can know God's will. It really is not difficult. If we want to know God's will and are willing to do it, not knowing what it is, we have the assurance that He will make it known to us. Abraham Lincoln said, "When the Almighty wants me to do something in particular, He has a way of letting me know it." God *wants* to speak to us!

I know a fine young man, the father of four children, who recently began to put his Christian faith to work in his job. He is a manufacturer's representative for a large plumbing and heating firm.

One day he told me that a product he was selling did not measure up to specifications. He felt that, as a Christian, he couldn't sell a product he knew was dishonestly advertised. He knew God had been speaking to Him. However, he was certain he would lose his job if he refused to sell this particular product. We prayed about it, and he told God he was willing to obey.

I saw Dave a few days later. He had spoken to the directors of the company he was representing and told them he was convinced that the product was not all it was advertised to be and that he, as a Christian, could not sell it.

The result of this act of faith came some weeks later. The company withdrew the product from its line, planning to work on it and make it what they had advertised. Dave was commended for his integrity and retained his position. But it might not have turned out so well. There is no guarantee. If we could be sure of the outcome, faith would not be necessary.

Nicholas Murray Butler says, "I divide the world into three classes — the few who make things happen; the many who watch things happen; and the overwhelming majority who have no notion of what happens."

We all want to belong to that class of people who "make things happen." There is a desperate need today for people of Christian faith — people who will make things happen by God's power, according to His will.

THE SIMPLICITY OF PRAYER

9. THE SIMPLICITY OF PRAYER

How To Pray

JESUS SAYS QUITE SIMPLY, *"Whatever* you ask in my name, I will do it." How many praying people really believe this? All too many pray with the same faith one has in a slot machine, "It won't cost too much, and I might hit the jackpot."

I am convinced that most of us really want to know how to pray. We want to discover the power of God, which is rightfully ours in Jesus Christ.

Prayer is conversation between two persons. Now conversation in itself is neither good nor bad. We all know what it is like to talk to The Gossip, The Bore, or The Crank. Such conversation is not helpful and at times is really harmful. Then there is the conversation that you have with the man who comes to read your water meter which is neither helpful nor harmful but polite routine. Conversation is what you make it. It can be irrelevant, or crucial, as in a midnight phone call to the doctor. It can be dull or stimulating. It can

be necessary and business-like or it can lead to deep relationships in friendship or even marriage.

In the same way prayer can be as meaningless as much of
our conversation, or it can be conversation between you and
God that is vital, exciting, and transforming.

Conversation always implies a relationship between two
or more persons. The quality of the conversation depends on
the kind of relationship that exists between the two. This can
be as impersonal as that between you and the voice that
answers the phone when you dial "O," or it can be as intimate
as the relationship between a husband and wife.

As Christians our prayers should be intimate conversations
with God, because through Jesus Christ we become children
and God becomes a loving father. And yet, how many sincere
people wake up every morning, meet God at the breakfast
table, and say some little jingle that rhymes to thank Him
for the food. If you spoke that way to your husband or wife
every morning, it would be grounds for divorce. It would be
an insult to speak that way to an intelligent person.

Yet God, though He is a Spirit, is a Person. Why talk to
Him as though He were a statue or a simple-minded child?
This is why Jesus warns us, "Do not use vain repetitions (or
empty phrases) as the heathen do; for they think that they
will be heard for their many words." You deny that God
is your Father when you talk to Him only in memorized
prayers or little sing-song jingles. A child's first words to his
earthly parents are not a sing-song jingle, but a meaningful
word or two conveying an honest request. Why should this
not apply when speaking to one's heavenly Parent? When a
child is old enough to be taught to pray, he is old enough to
learn that prayer is merely conversation with a heavenly
Father.

What does Jesus mean when He says, "Whatever you ask in my name, I will do it . . ."? He does not mean to pray using His name as a sign-off at the end of a prayer, but rather to pray in His name by experiencing Him as Lord and Saviour and through Him to experience God as Father. Believing that God exists is not the same as experiencing Him as Father. To experience Him is to enter into a new relationship with Him Person-to-person and to grow daily in this relationship.

The most important single factor in effective prayer is that the person praying be in the right relationship with God. How does one enter this right relationship? I can put it quite simply in three steps:

(1) Take an honest look at yourself. Admit that no matter how hard you try, you never do become the person you know God wants you to be.

(2) Give up the hopeless job of trying to remake your life. Believe that God came into the world in Jesus Christ just to help you become the person you ought to be and, down deep in your heart, would really like to be. In Jesus we not only see God's love for us, but in the living Christ we experience the power to change that God makes available to us now.

(3) Put yourself completely in God's hands. Surrender to Him not only your problems but also your most cherished plans for the future. Don't hold back a thing. Believe that by seeking first His Kingdom, all that you really need shall be given to you.

Guideposts for Effective Prayer. Once you are in the right relationship with God, the following guideposts will prove helpful in making your prayer life more effective:

With Whom Should I Pray? Part of your prayer life should

include prayer alone with God. Jesus said, "When you pray, go into your room and shut the door and pray to your Father who is in secret." Part of your prayer life should be with others. Jesus said, "If two of you agree on earth about anything they ask, it will be done for them by my Father in heaven. For where two or three are gathered in my name, there am I in the midst of them." Pray as a family. How else will your children learn to pray?

When Should I Pray? Pray in the morning. Give God your day and your troubles and put yourself at His disposal for service. Pray in the evening. Take an inventory of your day and then ask forgiveness where you failed and thank Him where He gave you power to overcome. Pray all day long — while working or walking or talking with others. Learn to pray short sentences all day long that ask for help or give thanks. Let God know that you know that He is there.

In What Position Should I Pray? Pray on your knees in the morning and at night. There is nothing magical about the position. It is just that it reminds you with whom you are talking when you are sleepy and your mind may wander. Pray in any position throughout the day. The main thing is that you pray. The position is not important. I have one friend who talks with God while driving to work in the morning. He imagines that God is sitting on the seat next to him and they talk about plans for the day.

Listen When You Pray. At least half of good conversation ought to be listening. Most of us ask God for advice and guidance and then never listen for an answer. Spend half of your prayer time in quiet listening. Learn to expect answers. Believe that God really wants to talk to you.

Respond Immediately to Guidance. Respond immediately to whatever guidance God gives you in prayer. Until you walk in the light of what you have, you will never get more light. God's guidance is like the light on a miner's hat which throws a beam six feet ahead. Unless you walk those six feet, you will never see more of the path before you. So God's guidance is step by step.

When Praying for Healing. When you are praying for someone who is sick, know that God does not send sickness. Believe that God wants to heal the person for whom you are praying. Assume this when you pray! Don't keep saying, "If it be Your will" in your prayers for healing of a person. Of course it is always implied in all your prayers. But pray believing that God loves that person more than you do and wants to make him well.

Be Positive When You Pray. Be positive when you pray, especially when praying for someone who is sick. Have a picture in your mind of that person already made well and whole and ask God to accomplish just that. This is where faith comes in. Faith is not a negative attitude where you cry out to God to prevent the worst from happening (and hence carry a picture of that person at his worst in your mind while you pray). Rather, faith is believing that God will heal and has already healed through the presence and power of Christ, even while you pray.

Pray Believing. Jesus says, "Therefore I tell you, whatever you ask in prayer, believe that you receive it and you will." This is what faith is. It is belief in the love and power of God to act. Jesus says in another place, "Whatever you ask in prayer, you will receive if you have faith."

Relax. Relax, both physically and spiritually, when you pray. One man says, "Don't pray hard. Pray easy. Prayer doesn't do it. God does it." Relaxed prayer takes faith. Faith is demonstrated by our trust. Our trust shows in our relaxation. A good technique to follow is to pray with your palms open and turned up, not with your fingers clenched together. Lift people and situations and yourself to God for help on your open palms.

Surrender. Surrender when you pray. Don't merely ask God for help. Give situations and people to God and trust Him. This underlies all prayer and is the most important single guidepost to remember. It is not enough to believe that God loves us and can help us. We must so trust Him that we let go of things and give them to Him.

There is a young mother I know whose little boy of five came down with meningitis. She stayed by his bed in the hospital, helping the nurses and praying constantly, but his fever of 106° continued. After more than thirty hours a nurse said that with the medication he was getting he should have responded in five to eight hours. She implied that there was no hope. With this, the mother got to her knees and surrendered the child to God, whom she knew loved him even more than she did. As his pain was unbearable, she put Bobby in God's hands and asked Him for quick death or quick recovery, believing that this was what a loving Father would want for His child. As she surrendered him to God's love, peace came to her instantly. But that is not all. Within the hour the boy's fever broke and healing came.

Sometimes it is easier to surrender another than to surrender one's self. Catherine Marshall, in the book *A Man Called Peter,* tells of being ill with tuberculosis. At first she rebelled and asked God, "Why?" Then in the long months that followed, as she read the New Testament accounts of Jesus' healing, she believed He was alive and with her and that the same power was still His. She prayed for healing but nothing happened. Finally she realized that she was not surrendered to God. She put herself completely in His hands, saying that she believed He could heal her if He wanted to, but that she was willing to be an invalid the rest of her life if that were how He could best use her. Immediately upon surrendering herself to God, the X-rays showed that she was recovering.

Believe these three simple facts when you pray and you can expect miracles:

(1) Believe that Christ loves you even more than you love yourself. The Cross is proof of this. (Read John 15:13.)

(2) Believe that all power is His, physically as well as spiritually. (Read Matthew 28:18.)

(3) Believe that He is right there with you when you pray. (Read Matthew 28:20.)

Build your prayers on these facts, and then your Lord says to you, "Whatever you ask in My name, I will do it."

"WHERE TWO OR THREE ARE GATHERED . . ."

10. "WHERE TWO OR THREE ARE GATHERED . . ."

The Power of Praying Together

THERE IS NOTHING intrinsically good about praying or beginning a prayer group. Prayers and prayer groups are what we make them, or what we let God make them.

A prayer group can be as much an escape from the real issues of life as a cocktail party. Jesus may be calling us to face certain facts, or to make right certain relationships, while we escape Him and His demands by busying ourselves with a cozy group of Christians who enjoy being together, praying for the world.

A prayer group can be another burden to an already full schedule of activities, that, far from giving life, crushes the life we have and makes living even more fragmented. A prayer group can be as irrelevant as reading an old telephone book, or as out of date as last year's Christmas card list. Prayer can be offered repeatedly for the same people and situations. This is a denial of faith. There is something wrong

about praying for the same things for the same people over
and over.

However, a prayer group can be the most relevant, vital,
powerful, and up-to-date appointment we keep all week.
Through a prayer group that is open to God, lives can be
changed and the whole course of human events altered. That
this has happened many times in the past is history. There is
no magic in just praying. Prayer doesn't change things. God
changes things.

A prayer group must be organic to be vital. The organizational part of its life should be kept to a minimum. The best
way to begin a family is to start with two people. Some of the
most powerful prayer groups have begun with just two
people meeting together for months, sometimes years, before
growth. One recent group I know began when a minister and
a newspaper editor promised God to begin a prayer group the
next morning at seven o'clock. That night two additional men
had their lives changed by God and the group doubled before
it had met once. However, it all began with two men.

We should not be alarmed when our group has "ups and
downs," for life has an ebb and flow. An organization may
never vary. Most church committees are like the Bureau of
Internal Revenue, that goes on and on with never a variation
even though the personnel changes. You can build a house but
not a tree. Life cannot be regimented.

The actual time spent in praying in a group is not the
important thing. The real issue is not how long our prayers
are, but how *real* they are — how *honest* they are — and how
much of ourselves is in them.

Sometimes you hear the comment, "Our prayer group
drifted into a Bible study." Now, none of us ever does enough
Bible study, but it is wrong when Bible study squeezes out

prayer and a relationship in depth with each other. Perhaps this shows a fundamental weakness in most of us in the Western world. We are more content-centered than we are life-centered. The East is concerned about "being truth," while we in the West are more concerned about "knowing truth." Jesus said, "I came that ye might have life," and the goal of both Bible study and prayer is Christ's life in us, not ideas about Him.

How we invite people to our prayer group reveals a great deal about what our group actually is. If we merely invite them to come and pray with us, we exclude all but those persons who seem to have a natural affinity for prayer. How many of Jesus' disciples enjoyed praying before He called them? It was the people with an affinity for prayer who crucified Jesus. The "needy" received Him gladly.

Prayer should never be the center of a prayer group. The true center is Jesus Christ and people's needs. Prayer is merely a link between the need and the answer. We should invite people to come and discover some answers for the needs in their own lives. Everyone has needs, and can be intrigued, especially if he has heard something from some of the members of the group about recent answers to their own needs.

Here are four points that will help make prayer alive in any prayer group:

(1) Prayer should be *realistic*. Christ's presence in a vital prayer group should make each person more aware of his own need for change, rather than the need for others to change. In almost every situation we are like the man complaining to the landlord about the noisy tenants upstairs who often stamped on the floor and shouted until after midnight. When asked if they bothered him, he replied, "No, I usually

stay up and practice the tuba until about that time every night, anyway."

Prayer should be realistic also in that we realize that changing our circumstances will not answer our problems. A new house and furniture will not change a marriage. Money to pay off a mortgage will not give life to a church. Health alone will not make a person happy.

(2) Prayer must be *honest*. We need to learn that God is not so concerned with our saying the "right" things as with our saying the "real" things. It was a turning point in my own life when I came to see that God did not expect me to say certain things in prayer, but rather waited for me to express my needs, even rebellion against Him, so that He could deal with me.

A young man was about to drop out of seminary. His devotional life had withered. He prayed only when he led worship occasionally in a little church. He was afraid to pray because he could not say the things he thought he ought to say to God honestly. When he discovered that God wanted him to pray about his lack of faith, his coldness of heart, his disinterest in prayer, a new relationship with God began.

(3) Prayer should be as *natural* as conversation, even though reverent. God is not stuffy and certainly does not want us to be stuffy with Him. Being formal and having a broken and a contrite heart are two different things. The language of prayer can be from the prayer book, but it can also be conversational. It is not how we pray, but what we pray about and the actual surrender to God of the things for which we pray that make the difference.

(4) Finally, we should develop a sense of *expectancy* as we pray. Hopeless prayers are the most pathetic things in the world. Real faith is expressed in expectancy.

When two or three are gathered together honestly, realistically, naturally, and expectantly, Christ can work miracles that heal cancers, heal homes, remove barriers, or bring spiritual awakening that touches countless lives. Anything is possible!

WHAT MAKES THE DIFFERENCE?

11. | WHAT MAKES THE DIFFERENCE?

Honesty Is the Only Policy

GOD IS NOT SHOCKED by our sins. There isn't a sin that any of us has committed, or is now practicing, that Jesus Christ did not deal with realistically in His life and sacrificially on the Cross. Jesus associated with call-girls, alcoholics, and chiselers. He didn't condone what they did. Nor did He leave them as He found them. But the record indicates that they enjoyed His company.

However, it is recorded in the fifth chapter of the Book of Acts that two very fine people — Ananias and Sapphira — dropped dead in His first church. They weren't drunks. As far as we know, he wasn't stepping out on her. They went to prayer meetings. They were more than tithers. But they were pretending something that wasn't true before God and His people. They didn't have to give a cent from the land they sold to the church, but they *pretended* to give it all when they actually gave only half.

Now God didn't kill them. The spiritual laws are such that when we are hypocrites, we cut ourselves off from the life God wants to give, and often we pick our own kind of death — a sudden coronary, as they might have had, or some slow death. But death is inevitable, whether physical, mental, psychic, or spiritual.

How accurate a picture do Ananias and Sapphira give us of our own lives and our own churches? Do I dare find out who I really am? Have I let anyone else know who I really am? The lie we live is probably only a lie we tell ourselves. Most people who get close to us surely see more than we think but are too polite to tell us what they see.

The neighborhood bar is possibly the best counterfeit there is to the fellowship Christ wants to give His Church. It's an imitation, dispensing liquor instead of grace, escape rather than reality, but it is a permissive, accepting, and inclusive fellowship. It is unshockable. It is democratic. You can tell people secrets and they usually don't tell others or even want to. The bar flourishes not because most people are alcoholics, but because God has put into the human heart the desire to know and be known, to love and be loved, and so many seek a counterfeit at the price of a few beers.

Christ wants His Church to be unshockable, democratic, permissive — a fellowship where people can come in and say, "I'm sunk!" "I'm beat!" "I've had it!" Alcoholics Anonymous has this quality. Our churches too often miss it.

The rebirth of a Biblical theology in most of the major denominations today has resulted in a commitment-centered message. I genuinely rejoice in it, but it's not enough. One more altar call, decision card, church officers' retreat, or campfire surrender won't do it. Something else is needed. *A fellowship must exist where committed people can begin to be honest with one another and discover the dimension of apostolic fellowship.*

It is interesting to see that a large portion of the secular, indifferent, irreligious part of our society today often has more reality and genuine concern for others than many church people.

There is a minimum of soul-stifling pretense on the part of many pagans. They cheat on their income tax and laugh about it on the golf course. They get drunk in front of their whole club. They tell their marital troubles in detail to their hairdresser. They talk honestly to their bartender; they talk deeply to their psychiatrist; and they talk indiscreetly in the locker room to each other. But there is a real openness and transparency that is healthy.

We all know what can happen when one of these open, honest pagans comes to a Billy Graham meeting or some similar place and there is a chance "to make a decision." When the statement, "Jesus Christ, take my whole life," is coupled with their honesty, we see them born in the Spirit right before our very eyes!

Commitment alone does not open the door for the Holy Spirit to empower us and to do His desired work in us. A second key is needed. We can call it "honesty" — a word seldom found in a theological word book or concordance. The Biblical word "confession" makes most Protestants today think of a little booth and a priest. This is not what the New Testament writers intended. They meant people being honest with God in the presence of others — and being honest with each other.

For the committed Christian who has missed the power of the Holy Spirit to become a new person, honesty with another about himself can remove the blocks and bring freedom and release. The Holy Spirit will come in, do His work, and give His gifts. He does not have to be coaxed or implored. When we make the conditions right and remove the blocks, He is immediately free to heal and help and empower.

When God has His way and we are liberated, we know it and the world knows it. He doesn't make us perfect. We still have to say "forgive me" daily. But we "walk in the light" with God, each other, and ourselves.

Honesty is essential to Christian growth. God keeps showing me that at heart I am a phony (another name for a sinner). I used to tell out-and-out "social" lies, but I have gotten beyond that (restitution was too painful!). I am much more subtle now. I can lie with the truth. I can project an image which is all based on fact, but which gives a totally false picture about me, my family, my work, or my church. But when we live the honest, open life in apostolic fellowship, God's people puncture those lies. It is costly, but therapeutic and liberating.

Honesty is God's way for a family of Christians to become a Christian family. In our first church, after graduating from seminary, my wife and I were both committed Christians, but we hadn't yet discovered a Christian marriage. Two other young married women began to meet with my wife — both members of our church. Over coffee one morning the three admitted for the first time how they were failing as wives and mothers. When they prayed together, Christ's healing began.

We three husbands saw and experienced this change in our wives and soon there were six committed people living in honest fellowship, meeting together each week. The group began to grow and divide. Inside of two years there were about a dozen groups like it meeting throughout the city, involving people from dozens of churches. But it all began when three girls over coffee said, "This is who I really am. I don't want to be like this any more. Jesus Christ, will You change me?"

Our children need to know who their parents really are. This gives them freedom to minister to us. One of our sons, when he was six, prayed one night at family devotions, "Lord, forgive us for running all over the country telling people about Jesus and then being so grumpy at home!" They pray for us and become an instrument of Christ's healing. Their faith then is in Jesus Christ Himself, not in a false picture of their parents' goodness.

Honesty is also the key to fellowship. The equation for New Testament Christianity is fourfold. "And they continued steadfast in the apostles' doctrine and fellowship, the breaking of bread and prayers" (Acts 2:42). Most churches are strong on doctrine, prayers, and communion. But the apostolic fellowship is missing. This isn't the only way to the renewal of the Church, but it's part of the whole pattern. A three-wheeled wagon can't go far. All four wheels are required for the church to be the Church.

Honesty is the key to personal effectiveness. God uses my confessed, redeemed sins more than all the theology and psychology I've learned. When I'm counseling just with sound Biblical theology, I never see "Biblical" results. The price needs to be paid in personal honesty.

The Bible is full of the theology of confession. It begins with Adam and runs through the institution of the Levitical priesthood, the experience of the Psalmist, the conviction of the prophets, and on into the New Testament. Even church history tells us that the Early Church practiced confession within the fellowship for the first four hundred years. Confession to a priest became an option, and remained an option from the fifth century until a Papal decree in the thirteenth century made it the only way. With the Protestant Reformation confession to God alone became the only way for many.

Today with the renewal of the Church centering in re-discovery of the lay minstry and small group fellowship, we are about to see on a large scale new facets of the old truth that honesty is the *only* policy.

THE CHURCH IN REVOLUTION

12. THE CHURCH
IN REVOLUTION

God's Strategy for Today

An English bishop once said, "Everywhere Paul went there was a revolution, but everywhere I go they serve tea." We Christians are called "to turn the world upside down," but too often we end up confessing our oneness with this bishop. God is doing new things in our time and we who want to be effective must not be afraid to follow Him down paths that may seem strange.

Over 2500 years ago the prophet Isaiah reported God as saying, "Remember not the former things nor consider the things of old. Behold, I am doing a new thing; now it springs forth. Do you not perceive it?"

God does not change. The heart and mind of God are eternal. Rebellion and loneliness in the heart of man remain the same in all ages. But God's strategy in the world changes from one generation to another, conditioned by the times, the places, the events, the culture, and all the variables of human life. Many different facets of God's strategy for today

117

have been observed and reported in the last few years. Let us look at a few.

A New Understanding of the Church. God is giving us a fresh understanding of the nature and the mission of His Church. In our time the Church has grown large and become prosperous. We know how to win members, raise budgets, erect buildings, organize and administrate effectively. But if the Church exists for the world, our very success undermines our mission and becomes an impediment.

We used to see the Church primarily as the clergy, with laymen helping with the chores, so that the clergy could get on to preaching the Gospel, helping people, making pronouncements, and attacking social evils. Now we see that laymen are God's primary instruments for helping individuals, for witnessing to the Gospel, and for attacking the forces of evil, while we clergy are to be their teachers and helpers.

If the Church exists for the world, and if laymen are the Church, then we in the Church need to experiment with new strategy. One church in California recruited fifteen of its most able men and assigned one clergyman to train these men intensively for two years. They were to be ordained as elders with the sole function of ministering outside the church — in the apartment buildings or neighborhoods where they lived, and in the factories and office buildings where they worked — with no teaching or organizational assignment in the church. When the Church thrusts its best men into the world in such a way even at the cost of weakening its own leadership, we see revolutionary Christianity. Churches, as well as individuals, must learn to lose their lives.

A New Strategy. Beginning with the Middle Ages, Christianity was thought of in terms of "Christendom," with the hope that the growing forces of Jesus Christ would gradually overcome the world numerically. But today the percentage of Christians in the world is actually shrinking and with it our whole concept of Christendom.

God is showing us again His original strategy, which comes with such newness in our day, that in Jesus Christ we are called to be leaven in society, not a massive force. We see here the wisdom of God, for *the revolutionary minority always has the advantage.* The strategy of infiltration is more effective than that of frontal attack.

There is a striking account in *The Ugly American* of an Asian country which had been occupied and controlled by the communists. A Roman Catholic priest from America gathered a dozen local Christians around him, and they began to meet secretly in the jungle to pray and think through a strategy of infiltration. In a very short time, God enabled them to overthrow the communist grip on their country and to produce an election that changed the government.

We need to see that two or three people in a neighborhood, or a dozen in a town, who pray and discuss strategy, can be God's agents for accomplishing His work in that place.

In a central Florida town there are two large neighboring churches. When the civil rights issue became crucial two years ago, one minister forced through an official statement of nondiscrimination against the will of his officers and members. The other minister resisted the pressure to produce a statement, but he quietly began to bring integrated groups into his church for conferences and meetings. To this day the first church has never had a Negro in it, though the pastor has been praised for his public stand, while the second has moved consistently over the last two years toward greater integration. To the latter, getting the job done was more important than wearing a hero's medal.

A New Center of Healing. The Church today is redis-
covering its authority for healing — physical, emotional, and
spiritual. Training in medicine and psychotherapy is important, but in addition to this we need communities of faith
and love where people are cared for deeply. Local churches
can and should be these communities.

I know of two rehabilitation centers, manned by relatively
untrained laymen, that are channels of God's healing for the
sick and emotionally disturbed. And I have personally seen
people who were not helped by individual therapy who were
brought to health through involvement with a small group of
laymen meeting each week.

I recently asked a professor of clinical psychology what
was the essential ingredient in training an effective therapist.
"Oh, that's easy," he said. "The people who become effective
are those whose lives are transparent to their patients." And
then he added sadly, "But we don't know how to put this
quality of openness and transparency into the people who
come for training."

The Church needs to move with boldness into this area, to
take responsibility for the emotionally disturbed, and to raise
up small groups whose members are willing to learn to love
and care deeply for one another.

At a recent conference in Oregon, a lovely young mother
stood up at the closing meeting to ask forgiveness of another
team member. "This is the first time that I have asked any-
body's forgiveness since I was seven years old," she confessed,
and turning to her husband asked, "Isn't that right, Dear?" He
nodded vigorously. "When I was six," she continued, "my
mother died. My father remarried and my stepmother hated
my sister and me. To make matters worse, I broke one of her
wedding presents and she hated me even more. My father

suggested I ask her forgiveness. I did and found that she not only wouldn't accept my apology but she hated me still more. I have never from that moment to this asked anyone's forgiveness.

"But at this conference I have discovered in the openness and the love that what I have heard in church all my life is true. I heard that God loves me as I am and believed it, but no one else has ever treated me as though he believed it. Now I know it's true; I am released and am even free to ask forgiveness when I am wrong." These are the kinds of miracles that should be taking place every day in every church — God working through ordinary people to bring release to others. This is normal Christianity.

A New Center of Authority. Each era has demanded a different center of authority through which God could confront the world. In the Dark Ages God used the very structure of the Church as the one organized, learned institution in a chaotic society. During the Reformation the Bible was rediscovered and became for Western Civilization the center of authority through which God spoke. Still later, preaching became God's primary means of confronting men.

But the world today is not impressed by the Bible, or by the Church, or by preaching. And we cannot confront a needy world with God's love primarily by these means. The climate of our time is one in which people listen most readily to laymen with whom they can identify. So as in the first century, ordinary laymen have become the center of spiritual authority.

Madison Avenue is discovering that the person down the street who is "just like me" is the person I will listen to. Much of our present-day advertising focuses on unknown women in laundromats, unknown truck drivers, or unknown students reporting the findings of dental tests.

A gifted pastor in South Dakota is much in demand as a speaker and evangelist. But he has discovered that teams of his own laymen going into other churches to witness are more effective in reaching people and aiding in renewal. These teams of laymen are not a schedule-stretcher for a busy parson, but actually a more generous and effective means of one church sharing its "new life" with other churches.

A New Language. Clinical reporting is a universal language in a way that concepts and theories are not. Truth can best be communicated not only to the pagan world but to other Christian groups if we stay on the level of experience.

If I talk about "sin" or "grace," I find great difficulty in communicating. But if I, as a father, talk about my failures in everyday living and about receiving a new kind of love from God for my children, I find that I am understood by the Christian and pagan father alike. We must learn to say, "Let me tell you what happened the other day," rather than, "I think this is what you should do." Clinical reporting is the language of the ecumenical movement at the grass roots.

A New Fellowship. God is helping His Church discover the reality of apostolic fellowship. The Church is meant to be a company of people as committed to one another as to Christ and to have, as in the first century, "all things in common." Worship on Sunday should grow out of a life shared during the week in small groups meeting for prayer, for nurture, and for encouragement in personal ministry.

Alcoholics Anonymous, which has its roots in the Church, is a good example of how God can use honest, open fellowship to bring people to reality and power, to keep them that way, and to help them reach out and share the good news with others in need.

A New Focus in Theology. Our generation has experienced a rebirth of Biblical theology and has recovered the fact that God's truth is revealed primarily in events rather than in concepts or systems or ideas.

God, in choosing the Hebrew people to be His first communicators to the world, chose a people whose language was not conceptual or philosophical. Hebrew is an action language which centers in verbs rather than adjectives, and the Bible is basically a chronicle of events rather than a handbook of principles or a systematic theology. So we must see the Bible as a record of what God has done and how man has responded.

If this is the nature of the Bible, it has profound implications for our witness today. Biblical preaching will stress the fact that God is acting now and will be illustrated with stories of present encounter. Martin Buber said, "Truth is I-thou and not I-it." Truth is a living God speaking to a man and acting in his life. The substance of faith is man's obedience and action. This event-theology lays the groundwork for the new authority of lay witness.

A New Evangelism. The new evangelism differs from the old in manner, means, and approach. The emphasis is more on person-to-person relationships than mass meetings, on laymen witnessing rather than clergymen preaching, and on love as the motivation for response rather than fear and guilt. These were Jesus' own methods.

When we see how Jesus treated the Samaritan woman who was living in adultery, we are staggered. He honored her theological discussions and treated her with love and respect. The result was that she confessed her sins, bore witness, and brought the whole town to meet Him.

The same thing was true of the hated collaborator and tax collector, Zacchaeus. Jesus honored him with a visit, respected him as a person, and ate at his table. As a result Zacchaeus said,

"I'm a terrible person. I've lied and I've stolen, but I will repay it four times over and give half my goods to the poor."

The truth about God revealed in Jesus Christ is like a coin with two sides — love and judgment. Both are true. Many well-meaning people confront the world saying that life without Jesus Christ is hell and leads to destruction. But we are finding that most people are all too aware of their wrong-doing but cannot admit it until they discover the unconditional love of God. We are discovering Jesus' own method that the truest way to produce "conviction of sin" is to declare and demonstrate to people, "God loves you just the way you are."

A friend of mine in a weekly luncheon group in New York reported that God was giving him a new freedom with people. "I've always been sticky and pious," he explained, "and have been unable to say anything to strangers except 'Do you know the Lord?' The other day I watched a woman feeding pigeons in Bryant Park and began to pray for her. I felt prompted to say to her, 'You remind me of Albert Schweitzer.' She was visibly shocked and said that people had called her many things during her years of feeding pigeons but never anything like that. What did I mean?"

My friend explained that Albert Schweitzer, the famous missionary, had a reverence for all living things because of his love for God. After such a gracious introduction he was able to talk naturally with this woman about God and His love and they parted friends.

One of the best ways to demonstrate God's love is to listen to people. Psychologists say it is impossible to distinguish intense listening from love. To care about a person enough to hear what he is saying may do more initially to introduce him to Christ than to tell him all kinds of things about God or yourself.

Intense listening is a way of affirming that God cares for people and is helping them even before they are aware of it. I have talked with hundreds of people from all kinds of circumstances. Whenever I suggest that God has been talking to them for a long time, even the most "unspiritual" invariably responds, "Yes, God has been talking to me. How did you know?"

Once a young British woman had the privilege of having dinner with two prime ministers in the same week, first Gladstone, then Disraeli. When a friend asked her what they were like, she replied, "When I was with Mr. Gladstone, I thought I was with the smartest man in the whole world. But with Mr. Disraeli, I thought I must be the smartest person in the world."

A New Style of Life. In recent years most active Christians have been identified either as those concerned about a personal faith or those involved in relevant social action. But to think that we must make a choice is heresy. God is raising up a new kind of disciple with a new style of life who is as much at home on a picket line as he is at a prayer meeting.

Any kind of social action that does not challenge individual commitment will not penetrate to the core of the problem. But any kind of personal relationship with Christ which does not involve us with a suffering world for which Christ died, is certainly an affront to the very Lord who is in His world suffering with all people.

A New Understanding of the World. Too often we think that if we are children of God through spiritual rebirth, we will automatically be in the will of God for daily life. Nothing could be further from the truth. Unfortunately many who don't know God may really be deeply involved in some aspect of His work, while sincere Christians may be working at cross-purposes to His will.

A clergyman came into his study one morning to find his little daughter gluing the pages of his new manuscript together into a hopeless mess. "What are you doing?" he shouted. The little girl replied, "I am helping you, Daddy." How often God's children have messed up His work!

What freedom we have when we see that God is already at work in the world. We can co-operate with Him and perhaps interpret what He is doing to our fellow workers who may not be Christian.

Several years ago a Christian youth group in East Berlin gave their free time to join with a communist youth group in building an orphanage. When the communists asked the Christians why they were helping them, knowing that Christianity and communism were at cross-purposes, the Christians replied, "You are doing God's work in the world and we want to help you." The communists were furious! But think of the impact of this witness. The Christians did not say that being a communist was God's purpose but that caring for homeless children is always God's purpose in the world.

The Bishop of Toronto said recently, "God does not spend much time in church!" What amazing insight! We Christians must come to see that it is *the world* for which Jesus Christ died and that we who belong to Him by faith must enter into the world to redeem it and change it simply because it is His world, whether the world knows it or not.

DATE DUE

DE 20 '9
